# The 'Pyrex' Book of Regional Cookery

Compiled by Diana Cameron-Shea

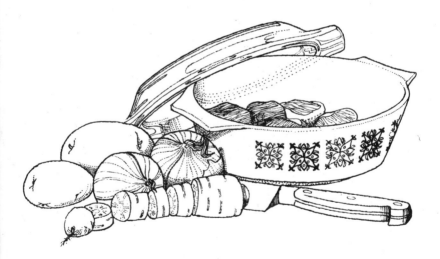

Drawings by Kate Simunek

# Acknowledgements

Corning Limited and Diana Cameron-Shea would like to acknowledge the help of the following in putting this book together:

The many friends and acquaintances who have helped to supply local recipes and variations on standard recipes.

Miss Barbara Duncanson for the information on Yorkshire curd cheese-cakes and Mrs Bell of South Cave, Yorkshire for her own recipe for curd cheesecake.

The Staff of the Corning Housecraft Recipe Service for locating recipes, typing and checking the manuscript. The home economist, Anne Ager, for testing and trying recipes.

All photography by John Lee.

'Pyrex' ® is the registered trade mark of Corning Limited, Sunderland, Tyne and Wear.

Hutchinson Benham Limited
3 Fitzroy Square London W1.

An imprint of the Hutchinson Group

London Melbourne Sydney Auckland
Wellington Johannesburg and agencies
throughout the world

First published 1977

©Text and photographs Corning Ltd
©Line drawings Hutchinson Benham 1977

Set in Monophoto Erhardt

Printed in Great Britain by
Sir Joseph Causton & Sons Ltd, London and Eastleigh

ISBN 0 09 129 5815

# Contents

# Introduction

People have different ideas of what a casserole is. Basically it is a dish which incorporates most of the main ingredients in one container. The ingredients can be meat, fish, poultry, game, offal or vegetables. Casserole cooking can be expensive or cheap according to your own particular wishes. You can add wines and cream to sauces to make them extra special or stick to basic recipes to keep costs down. Cheaper cuts and odd shapes of meat and poultry can be used since the long slow cooking tenderizes meats and the blend of herbs, spices and vegetables produces superb results. The best bonus for most cooks who favour casseroles is that preparation is quick and simple; once the dish is in the oven they are free to do other jobs, and using a casserole from which one can serve cuts down the washing up. Cooking for a number of people is easy with casseroles, only one main dish to prepare and produce, no last minute hasty preparation or trying to get several foods to the table at once and you can feed more people from a casserole than from many other types of dishes.

Puddings cooked in the oven alongside the casserole can make a complete meal without using any extra fuel. These puddings have been devised to cook in mainly medium ovens (gas mark 4 or 5, 350–375°F, 180–190°C) with the casseroles and will complement the dishes at the same time as saving on electricity or gas.

The casserole can be put in the centre of the oven for the first part of its cooking, but won't mind being moved down a shelf to make room for the pudding as it will still simmer nicely. This way both dishes can be ready together and the meal is cooked as economically as possible.

All the recipes in this book have been designed for ease of preparation. The step-by-step instructions are simple to follow for the beginner or the more experienced cook. All recipes use basic cooking equipment. The choice of a good casserole dish is important. Always use the correct size dish for the quantity of food you are preparing. Use good quality ovenware like 'Pyrex' ® which has all the guarantees you would expect from the name, and your results should be perfect. Good luck and good cooking!

All recipes are for four people unless otherwise stated. All spoon measurements are level unless otherwise stated.

# The
# South and West

*St. Michael's Mount*

Most of the recipes in this section were gathered during several holidays in the south and west country.

'Jeremy's pudding' is specially for a young man we know who loves this pudding anyway, but endeavours to eat most of the meringue before the rest of his family do!

Cornish cream casserole relies on a local item called 'dippy' which is a rich type of top-of-the-milk.

# Canterbury lamb casserole

1 lb (450gm) lamb for stewing
seasoned flour
1½ oz (37gm) butter
1 onion, sliced
1 tablespoon (15ml) lemon juice
1 tablespoon (15ml) chopped mint
   (or mint jelly)

1 pint (500ml) stock
seasoning
1 lb (450gm) carrots, scraped and
   sliced
1 lb (450gm) beans, sliced

Cut the lamb into 1-in (2.5-cm) cubes and toss in the seasoned flour. Fry quickly in the melted butter to brown all over. Turn into a 2½-pint 'Pyrex' casserole. Fry the onion in the fat and add to the lamb. Put the remaining flour into the fat and cook until golden. Mix the lemon juice, mint and water together and add gradually to the pan, stirring constantly. Season to taste and cook for 5 minutes. Place the carrots and beans in the casserole and pour over the liquid. Cook at gas mark 3, 325°F (170°C) for 1½ hours.

# Gooseberries and mackerel

4 oz (100 gm) butter
6 mackerel, cleaned, with heads
  removed
freshly ground nutmeg

$\frac{3}{4}$ lb (350 gm) fresh gooseberries
2 tablespoons apricot jam
parsley
grated rind of half a lemon

Melt half the butter in a large pan and quickly fry the fish for 1 minute on each side. Place these in a 5-pint 'Pyrex' casserole dish and sprinkle on nutmeg. Stew the gooseberries in a little water with the apricot jam until softened but not squashy. Pour the gooseberries over the mackerel and add the parsley and lemon rind. Cover and cook at gas mark 4, 350°F (180°C) for 45 minutes.

# Cornish under roast

1 lb (450 gm) steak
1 oz (25 gm) seasoned flour
2 onions, sliced

1 lb (450 gm) potatoes, peeled and
 quartered
1 pint (600 ml) stock
seasoning to taste

Cut the meat into strips, removing any excess fat. Dip into the seasoned flour and roll up the strips. Arrange most of the potato and onion in the base of a 2½-pint 'Pyrex' casserole dish. Set the rolled meat strips on top and arrange remaining potato and onion between the meat. Pour in the stock, season, cover and cook at gas mark 2, 300°F (150°C) for 1¼ hours. The lid may be removed after 1 hour to brown the potatoes.

# Cornish cream casserole

6 large fresh pilchards
1½ lb (700 gm) potatoes, peeled and
    sliced
seasoning

½ pint (300 ml) single cream
½ pint (300 ml) cream
    (off the top of the milk – 'dippy')

Clean the pilchards and remove heads and guts. Place in a 3½-pint 'Pyrex' casserole and arrange the sliced potatoes over the top. Season to taste. Mix the creams together and add to the casserole. Cover and cook at gas mark 3, 325°F (170°C) for 1 hour. *Serves 6.*

# Hampshire casserole

4 mackerel
8 plums, halved and stoned
1 teaspoon (5 ml) of fennel seeds
juice of half a lemon
½ pint (300 ml) dry cider

¾ lb (350 gm) potatoes, peeled,
    boiled and sliced
½ lb (225 gm) tomatoes, skinned
    and sliced

Remove heads from mackerel, clean and gut. Split and remove central bone. Wipe and place the plums inside each fish. Lay in the bottom of a 3-pint oblong 'Pyrex' casserole dish. Mix the fennel, lemon juice and cider together and pour over the fish. Cover the fish with the potatoes and top with the sliced tomatoes. Cook at gas mark 6, 400°F (200°C) for 30 minutes.

# New Forest casserole

½ lb (225 gm) boiled bacon
2 large onions
seasoning
1 rabbit, jointed

1 oz (25 gm) flour
½ teaspoon (2.5 ml) mixed herbs
1 pint (600 ml) herb stock

Cut the ham into slices and arrange in the bottom of a 3½-pint 'Pyrex' casserole. Slice the onions and place half of the onions over the bacon. Season to taste and add the rabbit joints. Dredge with the flour and herbs. Then add the rest of the onion and the remaining slices of bacon. Pour over the herb stock and cook at gas mark 3, 325°F (170°C) for 2 hours. *Serves 6.*

# South Down casserole

1 oz (25 gm) butter
1 lb (450 gm) mutton, cut into
  cubes
1 oz (28 gm) seasoned flour
1 onion, peeled and chopped

2 lettuces, cut into pieces
1¼ fl oz (40 ml) of sherry
¾ pint (450 ml) brown stock
8 oz (225 gm) green peas

Melt the butter in a pan. Turn the mutton in the seasoned flour and sear quickly in hot fat. Add the onion and cook for 5 minutes. Place one of the lettuces in the bottom of a 2½-pint greased 'Pyrex' casserole and lay the onions and mutton on this. Mix the rest of the flour into the fat and stir well. Add the sherry and stock and cook, over a low heat, until the mixture begins to thicken. Place the rest of the lettuce on top of the meat and pour over the sauce. Cook for 1½ hours at gas mark 4, 350°F (180°C). Remove from oven, add the peas, return to the oven and cook for a further 20 minutes.

# Mounts Bay crab

½ lb (225 gm) fresh cooked crabmeat
¼ lb (100 gm) mushrooms, sliced
2 hard-boiled eggs, sliced
1 tablespoon (15 ml) parsley, chopped
2 teaspoons (10 ml) lemon juice

1 onion, peeled and finely chopped
1½ oz (37 gm) butter
1½ oz (37 gm) flour
½ pint (300 ml) milk
seasoning to taste
2 oz (50 gm) fresh breadcrumbs
1½ oz (37 gm) grated cheese

Place crabmeat, mushrooms, eggs and parsely in 4 8-ounce 'Pyrex' casseroles. Sprinkle over the lemon juice. Cook the onion in the melted butter until soft, stir in the flour and gradually add the milk. Season to taste. Stir over a low heat until thickened. Pour over the contents of the casseroles and mix together. Add a little more milk if necessary. Sprinkle breadcrumbs on top. Cover and cook at gas mark 5, 375°F (190°C) for 30 minutes. Remove lids and add the grated cheese over the top of the food. Return, uncovered, to the oven for a further 15 minutes.

# Rich salmon and shrimp pie

1½ lb (700 gm) fresh salmon
3 hard boiled eggs, chopped
8 oz (225 gm) peeled shrimps or
  prawns
1-2 tablespoons (15–30 ml) grated
  onion
3 tablespoons (45 ml) parsley,
  chopped
salt, pepper, paprika

1 pint Bechamel sauce:
  3 oz (75 gm) butter
  1 oz (25 gm) flour
  1 pint (600 ml) milk
  salt
  pepper
2 oz (57 ml) white wine
creamy mashed potatoes

Remove skin and bones from salmon and cut into cubes. Place in a 3-pint oblong 'Pyrex' casserole with the eggs, shrimps, onion, parsley, salt, pepper and paprika and mix together. Make Bechamel Sauce by melting the butter in a saucepan, then add the flour and stir well. Gradually stir in milk and heat very gently until sauce thickens. Add the wine and pour over the salmon mixture in the casserole. Cover and cook at gas mark 6, 400°F (200°C) for 15 minutes. Remove the lid and pipe creamed potato around the edge of the salmon mixture. Cover salmon mixture with an oblong of buttered grease-proof paper and return to the oven for a further 15–20 minutes until the potato has browned.

# Jeremy's pudding

$\frac{3}{4}$ pint (450 ml) milk
rind from 1 lemon
$\frac{1}{2}$ oz (12 gm) butter
2 oz (50 gm) caster sugar
4 oz (100 gm) breadcrumbs
2 egg yolks

4 tablespoons (60 ml) strawberry
  jam
3 egg whites
6 oz (150 gm) caster sugar for
  meringue

Heat the milk gently, and add the lemon rind. Allow to infuse for a few minutes, then strain the milk into a bowl. Dissolve into it the butter and sugar and then stir in the breadcrumbs. Leave to cool, then stir in the egg yolks, mixing thoroughly. Turn into a greased general-purpose 'Pyrex' oven dish and leave to stand for 30 minutes. Bake at gas mark 5, 375°F (190°C) for 30 minutes until set. Spread the top with jam. Whisk all the egg whites until very stiff and fold in the caster sugar. Pipe on top of the pudding and put back in the oven for a further 10 minutes until lightly browned.
*Serves 6.*

# Warming baked apples

6 oz (150 gm) seedless raisins
6 large cooking apples
3 tablespoons (45 ml) brown sugar

1 teaspoon (5 ml) mixed orange and
   lemon peel, grated
1½ oz (37 gm) butter
½ bottle sweet white wine

Place the raisins in a basin and soak in the wine for 20 minutes. Meanwhile wash and core the apples, taking care not to pierce the blossom end. Place in a greased 'Pyrex' square roasting dish and fill the holes with the raisins, sugar and grated orange and lemon peel. Place a dot of butter on top of each apple and slowly pour the wine over. Bake for 1 hour at gas mark 5, 375 F (190°C) until apples are tender, basting occasionally to keep moist. *Serves 6.*

# The East

*Burnham Market*

The east of England is famous for its vegetable produce, its fish and poultry. The dishes in this section are drawn from mostly local recipes supplied by friends and relatives.

However we have adapted some restaurant dishes which were eaten and enjoyed. 'Spilsby bacon casserole' is a dish made by a friend's mother who lives in Spilsby and which she has kindly allowed us to print. 'Marrow casserole' is an unusual method of cooking marrow and is useful to pop into the oven with the Sunday roast to provide a hot vegetable dish – it also avoids the effort of eating one's way through a mammoth vegetable marrow in one go. You can re-heat 'Marrow casserole' simply by popping it back in the oven.

2 oz (50 gm) butter
2 large onions, sliced
$\frac{1}{4}$ of a green pepper, chopped
1 celery stalk, chopped
2 tomatoes, peeled
3 lb (1350 gm) turkey, skinned, off
   the bone and cut into pieces

salt and pepper
6 fl oz (780 ml) stock
$2\frac{1}{2}$ fl oz (75 ml) brandy
$\frac{1}{4}$ pint (150 ml) single cream
2 tablespoons (30 ml) parsley,
   chopped

Melt the butter in a frying pan and fry the onions, green pepper, celery and tomatoes for 4–5 minutes. Remove from the pan and place in the bottom of a $2\frac{1}{2}$-pint oval 'Pyrex' casserole. Season turkey with salt and pepper and fry in the hot fat until browned. Remove pan from the heat and stand to one side. Heat the brandy in a small pan and flame. Pour immediately over the turkey pieces. When the flames die down, add the stock and the cream. Pour this mixture into the casserole, cover and cook at gas mark 4, 350°F (180 C) for 2 hours. Remove from oven and sprinkle with chopped parsley before serving.

# Lincolnshire oxtail
## with dumplings

2½ lb (1125 gm) oxtail, jointed
1½ oz (37 gm) flour, salt and pepper
2 oz (50 gm) fat
2 bacon rashers
1 large onion, chopped
1 carrot, chopped
2 sticks celery

1½ pints (900 ml) beef stock
bouquet garni
**Dumplings**
6 oz (150 gm) self raising flour
3 oz (75 gm) shredded suet
1 tbl.sp. (15 ml) onion, chopped
water

Trim as much fat as possible from the oxtail then toss the pieces in seasoned flour. Melt the fat in a frying pan and fry the oxtail and chopped bacon until browned. Transfer into a 5-pint oblong 'Pyrex' casserole. Fry the onion, carrot and celery in the frying pan for a few minutes then stir in the remaining flour. Lower the heat and gradually add the stock. Bring to the boil, stirring continuously until the sauce thickens. Pour over the oxtail in the casserole, add bouquet garni, cover and cook at gas mark 2, 300°F (150°C) for 4 hours.

Prepare the dumplings by mixing the flour, suet and onion in a bowl and binding together into a soft dough with a little water. Form dumpling mixture into about 10 small balls and add to the casserole. Cover and cook for a further 15 minutes at a higher heat, gas mark 6, 400°F (200°C). Remove the lid and cook for another 10 minutes until the dumplings are browned. *Serves 6.*

# Lowestoft casserole

8 plaice fillets
2 teaspoons (10 ml) made mustard
4 oz (100 gm) mushrooms, sliced
1 small onion, thinly sliced
1 oz (25 gm) seasoned flour

1 oz (25 gm) butter
$\frac{1}{4}$ pint (150 ml) white wine
$\frac{1}{4}$ pint (150 ml) herb stock
$\frac{1}{4}$ pint (150 ml) single cream
paprika

Wash and dry the plaice. Spread each fillet with the mustard and lay some slices of mushrooms along the fish. Roll up the fillets starting at the tail with the mushrooms innermost. Pack into the lid of a 5-pint oblong 'Pyrex' casserole. Sprinkle the rest of the mushrooms and the thinly sliced onion over the fish. Melt the butter in a saucepan and add the flour. Blend well with a wooden spoon and cook over a low heat until this mixture turns golden brown. Remove from heat and add the wine, stock and cream gradually. Return to the heat and cook for 5 minutes, stirring constantly. Do not boil. Pour over the fish and cover with the bottom of the casserole. Cook at gas mark 4, 350°F (180°C) for 25 minutes. Sprinkle with paprika before serving.

# Spilsby bacon casserole

$\frac{3}{4}$ oz (20 gm) butter
4 1-in thick rashers lean belly
  of pork
$\frac{1}{2}$ oz (12 gm) seasoned flour
1 onion, sliced

1 small white cabbage
$\frac{1}{2}$ pint (300 ml) dry cider
1 tablespoon (15 ml) brown sugar
seasoning

Melt the butter in a heavy frying pan. Roll the pork rashers in the seasoned flour and fry quickly in the hot fat for a few minutes. Add the chopped onion and cook until soft. Wash and shred the cabbage into 1-in (2.5-cm) thick strips. Place in a layer on the bottom of a 3-pint clear 'Pyrex' casserole. Add a layer of onions and a rasher of pork. Continue layering and finish with a layer of cabbage. Add the remaining seasoned flour to the fat and cook for a few minutes. Remove from heat and add the cider and brown sugar. Return to a low heat and stir until hot and the sugar is dissolved. Season to taste and pour into the casserole. Cover with the lid and cook at gas mark 4, 350°F (180°C) for 2 hours.

# Country dumpling casserole

1 lb (450 gm) lamb's liver
1 oz (25 gm) seasoned flour
2 tablespoons (30 ml) oil
8 oz (225 gm) sliced onions

4 bacon rashers
4 oz (100 gm) button mushrooms
$\frac{3}{4}$ pint (450 ml) chicken stock
soy sauce

**Dumplings**
4 oz (100 gm) self raising flour
1 teaspoon (5 ml) dry mustard
salt and pepper

2 oz (50 gm) suet
parsley, chopped
water

Wash the liver, dry and cut into thin chunks. Coat each piece with seasoned flour. Heat the oil in a frying pan and fry the onions and chopped bacon until lightly browned. Add the liver pieces, mushrooms and soy sauce and stir gently for a few minutes. Stir in the remaining flour, lower the heat and gradually blend in the stock. Bring to the boil and simmer for 2 minutes, stirring continuously. Transfer the mixture into a 3-pint 'Pyrex' casserole, cover and cook for 25 minutes at gas mark 4, 350°F (180°C).

Prepare the dumplings by mixing the flour, mustard, salt, pepper, suet and parsely in a bowl. Bind with a little water and roll into about 8 small balls, on a floured board. Add to the casserole and return to the oven for a further 30 minutes until cooked through.

# Norfolk cod in cider

1 lb (450 gm) cod fillets
$\frac{1}{2}$ pint (300 ml) dry cider
$\frac{1}{2}$ lb (225 gm) potatoes, peeled,
  sliced and grated

2 firm tomatoes, skinned and sliced
seasoning
1 small onion, chopped

Cut the cod fillets into serving-size pieces. Place in a $2\frac{1}{2}$-pint 'Pyrex' casserole. Heat the cider in a pan with the potatoes and tomatoes for 5 minutes, season and pour over the fish. Sprinkle the onion over this, cover and cook at gas mark 4, 350°F (180°C) for 30–40 minutes.

# Cambridge hare

1 hare
2 onions, peeled and sliced
1 oz (25 gm) fat for frying
1½ oz (37 gm) seasoned flour
8 oz (225 gm) carrots, scraped
  and sliced

½ pint (300 ml) stock
½ pint (300 ml) beer
1 teaspoon (5 ml) sage
1 teaspoon (5 ml) parsley, chopped
1 teaspoon (5 ml) nutmeg

Skin and clean the hare. Cut into joints. Fry the onions in the hot fat until soft and place in a 5-pint 'Pyrex' casserole. Turn the hare in the seasoned flour and fry quickly in the hot fat until golden brown. Place in the casserole and add the carrots. Add the remaining seasoned flour to the fat and work the two together with a wooden spoon. Mix the stock, beer, herbs and nutmeg and add this to the flour mixture. Cook until thickened and smooth. Pour over the hare and cover the dish. Cook at gas mark 4, 350°F (180°C) for 2½ hours.

# Marrow casserole

½ oz (12 gm) butter
1 large onion, peeled and sliced
1 medium vegetable marrow
¼ teaspoon (1.2 ml) thyme

¼ teaspoon (1.2 ml) basil
¼ teaspoon (1.2 ml) sage
seasoning
2 tablespoons (30 ml) of water

Melt the butter in a frying pan and fry the onion gently until soft. Cut the marrow into 1-in (2.5-cm) thick slices and arrange in a lightly greased 2½-pint 'Pyrex' casserole. Mix the herbs and seasoning into the onion, place on top of the marrow and add the water. Cover and cook at gas mark 3, 325°F (170°C) for 40 minutes.

*Note:* There is no stock in this recipe as the marrow makes its own liquid during cooking.

# Duck with Madeira

4 lb (1800 gm) duck
2 oz (50 gm) seasoned flour
1 oz (25 gm) butter
4 rashers of bacon, chopped
1 large onion, sliced
$\frac{1}{2}$ pint (300 ml) stock made
   from giblets

$\frac{1}{2}$ pint (300 ml) Madeira
1 teaspoon dried sage
$\frac{1}{2}$ lb (225 gm) open mushrooms,
   sliced
chopped parsley to decorate

Clean the duck. Coat in half the seasoned flour and stand on a rack in the base of a 'Pyrex' chicken casserole. Prick all over with a meat skewer and sprinkle with sage. Roast at gas mark 6, 400°F (200°C) for $\frac{3}{4}$ hour. Remove the duck and the rack from the casserole and tip off the fat. Fry the bacon and onions until soft in the butter and stir in the remaining flour. Add the stock mixed with the Madeira. Season to taste and cook for 1 minute. Replace the duck in the casserole. Sprinkle the mushrooms over the duck and pour over the sauce. Cover and cook at gas mark 3, 325°F (170°C) for $1\frac{1}{2}$ hours. Garnish with chopped parsley when ready to serve.

# Fruity bread and butter pudding

6 large slices of bread, thinly sliced
1½ oz (37 gm) butter
3 eggs
2½ oz (62 gm) caster sugar
¾ pint (450 ml) milk

1 oz (25 gm) currants
1 oz (25 gm) sultanas
1 oz (25 gm) raisins
mixed spices

Spread the bread with butter and cut off crusts. Cut into triangles. Make the custard: whisk the eggs and 1½ oz (37 gm) caster sugar together in a large bowl. Warm the milk slightly and pour gradually into the egg mixture, whisking continually. Then butter an oblong 1½-pint 'Pyrex' pie dish and line with the bread triangles. Fill with alternate layers of mixtures of the dried fruits and remaining bread, ending with a layer of bread. Sprinkle the remaining sugar over. Strain all the egg custard over and sprinkle with the mixed spices. Bake for 30 minutes at gas mark 3, 325°F (170°C) until slightly browned.

# Pumpkin pie

2 lb (900 gm) cooking apples, peeled and sliced
1½ pints (900 ml) cooked and drained pumpkin
8 oz (225 gm) sugar
½ teaspoon (2.5 ml) ground cinnamon
½ teaspoon (2.5 ml) nutmeg, grated
1 tablespoon (15 ml) crystallized ginger, sliced
12 oz (350 gm) puff pastry
beaten egg
little caster sugar

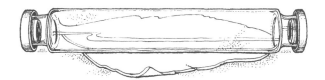

Mix the apples and the pumpkin, add the sugar, spices and ginger. Place in a 2-pint 'Pyrex' oval pie dish. Cover with the puff pastry. Decorate with shapes cut from pastry trimmings and brush with beaten egg, and dust with a little caster sugar. Bake for 30–35 minutes, gas mark 6, 400°F (200°C). *Serves 6.*

# The Midlands

*Canal scene*

To those of us who only journey up the M1 occasionally, the Midlands seems an area of factories, chimneys and industrial complexes. The other side of this picture is of rich agricultural areas yielding much beef and pork.

'Evenlode veal' is a special recipe from a farmer's wife near Shipston and the unusual combination of prunes and beef is from a 'legal eagle' and keen cook who lives near Loughborough. 'Chocolate rum pudding' is developed from a chocolate recipe, given to us by a local company specializing in sweets and chocolates.

1 oz (25 gm) butter
1 large onion, chopped
2 celery stalks, chopped
1 large can of baked beans

5 beefburgers
1 teaspoon (5 ml) mixed herbs
2 tablespoons (30 ml) breadcrumbs
3 oz (75 gm) Cheddar cheese, grated

Melt the butter and fry the onions and celery until soft. Place in the bottom of a 2-pint round 'Pyrex' casserole. Pour the baked beans on top and lay the beefburgers in the casserole. Sprinkle with a mixture of herbs, breadcrumbs and cheese. Cook, uncovered, at gas mark 4, 350°F (180°C) for 45 minutes.

# Evenlode veal

1½ lb (700 gm) stewing veal
1 oz (25 gm) seasoned flour
2 oz (50 gm) butter
1 onion, chopped
1 leek, chopped
4 tomatoes, peeled, seeded and
quartered

8 oz (225 gm) mushrooms, sliced
¼ pint (150 ml) white wine
¼ pint (150 ml) herb stock
1 teaspoon (5 ml) garlic salt
salt and pepper

Wipe the meat and cut into 1-in (2.5-cm) cubes, turn in seasoned flour. Heat the butter in a frying pan and fry the onion and leek until soft. Add the meat and fry until golden. Place in a 4¼-pint 'Pyrex' casserole and add the tomatoes and mushrooms. Stir the remaining flour into the fat and cook for 2 to 3 minutes. Gradually add the wine, stock and garlic salt. Season to taste and bring to the boil, stirring continuously. Cover the casserole and cook at gas mark 4, 350°F (180°C) for 1¼ hours.

# Broxtowe kidneys

1 lb (450 gm) lamb's kidneys,
cleaned and skinned
seasoned flour
1 oz (25 gm) fat for frying

2 onions, chopped
4 rashers of bacon
¼ pint (150 ml) stock

Remove the cores from the kidneys and slice. Turn in seasoned flour and fry in fat. Arrange in a 2-pint 'Pyrex' casserole and cover with chopped onions and chopped bacon rashers. Pour over the stock and cover. Cook at gas mark 4, 350°F (180°C) for 40 minutes.

Serve with broad beans and boiled potatoes.

# Marinated rabbit in red wine

| | |
|---|---|
| 1 large rabbit | salt and pepper |
| 4 oz (100 gm) bacon | 1 pint (600 ml) red wine |
| 2 tablespoons (30 ml) olive oil | 1 pint (600 ml) stock |
| 2 onions, sliced | $\frac{3}{4}$ oz (20 gm) cornflour |

**Marinade**

| | |
|---|---|
| $\frac{1}{4}$ pint (150 ml) red wine vinegar | few juniper berries |
| 3 tablespoons (45 ml) olive oil | 1 bay leaf |
| 1 onion | black pepper, marjoram, thyme |
| 2 cloves garlic | |

Cut the rabbit into pieces and place in marinade for a day in the refrigerator. Thinly cut the bacon into strips and fry in the oil, adding the onion, until brown. Remove and add the dried rabbit pieces and fry until lightly browned. Put these, the bacon and onion into a 3-pint 'Pyrex' casserole and season. Strain the marinade, place in a saucepan and boil until it has nearly evaporated, then add the wine. Boil again then add the stock. Pour this into the rabbit mixture, cover and cook for 1½ hours in a fairly hot oven gas mark 5, 375°F (190°C). When the rabbit is tender, skim off the fat and drain off the sauce. Mix the cornflour with a little water and add to the sauce. Bring to the boil and cook for a few minutes. Pour over the rabbit and serve.

# Casseroled beef
## with prunes and wine

½ lb (225 gm) onions
½ lb (225 gm) carrots
large piece of bacon rind or some
    lean scraps of bacon
1 oz (25 gm) fat
2 lb (900 gm) piece of lean beef,
    sliced

½ lb (225 gm) prunes
½ level teaspoon (2.5 ml) salt
½ pint (300 ml) red wine
½ lb (225 gm) noodles
Parmesan cheese, grated

Peel and chop onions and carrots, wash the bacon rind. Melt the fat in a deep saucepan. Fry the meat in it until brown all over. Remove the meat and place in a 5-pint 'Pyrex' casserole; put the bacon rind in the bottom and the vegetables and prunes on top; add the seasoning and wine. Cover and cook gently for 2½ to 3 hours at gas mark 2 or 3, 300°F (150°C), until the meat is tender. Just before dishing-up time boil the noodles in salted water. Drain and arrange the slices in the middle of the noodles and put the vegetables and prunes and sauce round it. Sprinkle the noodles with cheese and serve.

# Tewkesbury hot pot

2 lb (900 gm) bacon forehock
2 medium carrots, sliced
8 oz (225 gm) turnips, cubed
2 celery sticks, chopped
1 lb (450 gm) onions, sliced

1 lb (450 gm) potatoes, cubed
1 pint (600 ml) stock
1 small packet frozen or
    4 oz (100 gm) fresh peas

Put the bacon in a saucepan and cover with cold water. Bring to the boil and drain to remove excess salt. Cool for a few minutes and then remove rind. Place in a 4¼-pint 'Pyrex' casserole dish with the carrots, turnips, celery, onions and potatoes. Pour in the stock and cover with a lid. Cook at gas mark 5, 375°F (190°C) for 1¾ hours. Add the peas and cook for a further 15 minutes.

# Evesham chicken

2 oz (50 gm) butter
3 lb (1350 gm) chicken, cut into
  serving-size pieces
1 oz (25 gm) seasoned flour
1 onion, chopped
2 red-skinned eating apples,
  cored and sliced

$\frac{3}{4}$ pint (450 ml) dry cider
2 teaspoons (10 ml) of mixed herbs
salt and pepper
$\frac{1}{4}$ pint (150 ml) single cream
1 tablespoon (15 ml) parsley,
  chopped

Melt the butter in a frying pan and turn the chicken in the seasoned flour. Fry quickly, on all sides, in the hot fat. Place in a 5-pint 'Pyrex' casserole. Fry the onion and apples in the fat and then add these to the casserole. Add the remaining flour to the fat and cook for 2–3 minutes. Gradually add the cider and herbs, season to taste. Remove from the heat and stir in the single cream. Pour over the chicken and cover. Cook at gas mark 5, 375°F (190°C) for 1$\frac{1}{4}$ hours. Serve in the casserole lid. Garnish with chopped parsley.

# Oxfordshire ham and vegetables

1 large potato, thinly sliced
4 sticks of celery, chopped
1 large onion, sliced
1 green pepper, sliced
4 gammon steaks

1 medium can mushroom soup
seasoning
1 oz (25 gm) brown breadcrumbs
½ oz (12 gm) melted butter

Place a layer each of vegetables and gammon in a 3-pint oblong 'Pyrex' casserole. Season soup with salt and pepper and pour over vegetables and ham. Cover and cook at gas mark 4, 350°F (180°C) for 1 hour. Just before serving, toss the crumbs in melted butter and sprinkle over the top of the ham.

2 lb (900 gm) chicken giblets
12 oz (350 gm) cooked rice
2 spring onions, chopped
2 sticks of celery, chopped

pinch of paprika
seasoning
1 oz (25 gm) butter
6 fl oz (180 ml) herb stock

Wash fresh giblets and cut into small pieces. Place in a $4\frac{1}{4}$-pint oval 'Pyrex' casserole with rice. Add the onions, celery and paprika. Season to taste. Dot with butter and pour over stock. Cook at gas mark 3, 325°F (170°C) for 2 hours.

# Chocolate rum pudding

3 oz (75 gm) self-raising flour
1 oz (25 gm) cocoa
3 oz (75 gm) chocolate, chopped
2 tablespoons (30 ml) rum
1 oz (25 gm) fresh white
   breadcrumbs

3 oz (75 gm) soft margarine
3 oz (75 gm) caster sugar
2 eggs
little milk, if required

Sieve the flour and cocoa into a bowl; add remaining ingredients and beat together for about 2 minutes until well blended. If necessary, add a little milk to make a soft dropping consistency. Turn mixture into a greased 1½-pint 'Pyrex' pudding basin and cover with greased foil or greaseproof paper. Steam for 1¾ hours. Turn out of the basin and serve with custard or cream. *Serves 6*.

# Plum Crumble

1 large can of plums
6 oz (150 gm) self-raising flour
3 oz (75 gm) butter or margarine
2–3 oz (50–75 gm) demerara sugar

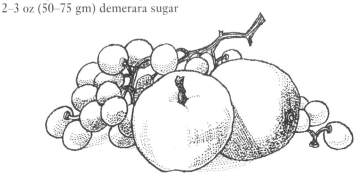

Drain the plums, put plums and 4 tablespoons of their juice into a 2-pint oval 'Pyrex' pie dish. Sieve the flour into a bowl and rub in the butter until the texture of coarse crumbs. Stir in the demerara sugar and sprinkle evenly over the plums. Bake at gas mark 5, 375°F (190°C) for 35–40 minutes. Serve with cream or custard. *Serves 6.*

# The Yorkshire Ridings

*Thwaite*

After some very enjoyable trips to all the Yorkshire Ridings and sampling most of the dishes gathered for this section we are firmly convinced that many of the best cooks in the country come from Yorkshire.

Having been told often by a friend now living in London that cheesecake, as many southerners know it, bears no relation to the delectable ones produced in Yorkshire, we wrote to the local paper in Hull asking for a good recipe. The reply was amazing, not only several lovely recipes but three curd cakes to sample as well. The one we have used is Mrs Bell's recipe. It is only a pity we could not print all the others we also received.

# Veal and lemon casserole

2 lb (900 gm) pie veal
2 tablespoons (30 ml) oil
2 carrots
1 lb (450 gm) tomatoes
2 lemons
2 onions, chopped

bouquet garni
wineglass of white wine
  (sweet wine may be used
  according to taste)
salt and pepper
chopped parsley

Trim veal and cut into even size pieces. Fry in oil until browned. Transfer to a 3-pint 'Pyrex' casserole and add chopped carrots, peeled and quartered tomatoes, the juice and most of the grated rind of two lemons, onions, bouquet garni, wine, parsley and seasoning. Cook at gas mark 4, 350°F (180°C) for 1½–2 hours. When meat is tender, check seasoning and garnish with remaining lemon rind.

# Country parsnips

12 parsnips
seasoning
$\frac{1}{2}$ oz (12 gm) butter

1 oz (25 gm) brown sugar
half a lemon
6 rashers of bacon

Top, tail and scrape the parsnips and boil in slightly salted water until cooked but not soft. Cut in half lengthways and place in a 3-pint 'Pyrex' oblong casserole dish. Season to taste and dot with the butter. Sprinkle over the sugar and the juice and grated peel of the lemon. Top with the bacon slices and cook, uncovered at gas mark 5, 375°F (190°C) for 20 minutes.

# Glazed carrots

1 lb (450 gm) carrots
$\frac{1}{4}$ pint (150 ml) water
2 oz (50 gm) brown sugar

3 oz (75 gm) butter
chopped parsley for garnish

Wash and scrape the carrots and cut into four lengthways and lay in a 2-pint 'Pyrex' casserole dish. Combine the water, sugar and butter in a pan and cook until the sugar is dissolved. Pour over the carrots, cover and cook at gas mark 4, 350°F (180°C) for 1 hour. Sprinkle with chopped parsley.

# Craven beef casserole

2 lb (900 gm) rump steak
2 oz (50 gm) seasoned flour
1½ oz (37 gm) fat for frying
1 pint (600 ml) tomato juice
2 teaspoons (10 ml) Worcestershire sauce
2 tablespoons (30 ml) made English mustard
1 teaspoon (5 ml) carraway seeds
seasoning
4 medium onions, peeled and cut into quarters
6 medium potatoes, peeled and halved
8 oz (225 gm) green peas

Cut meat into 2-in (5-cm) cubes. Turn in seasoned flour and brown in the hot fat. Turn into a 5-pint 'Pyrex' casserole. Stir the remaining flour quickly into the fat. Gradually add the tomato juice, Worcestershire sauce, mustard and carraway seeds. Simmer for 5 minutes and season to taste. Pour over the meat. Arrange the vegetables, except the peas around the meat, cover and cook at gas mark 4, 350°F (180°C) for 1¾ hours. Add the peas and cook for a further 20 minutes.

#  Sour cream potatoes

1½ oz (37 gm) butter, melted
2 eggs, beaten
14 fl oz (420 ml) sour cream
1 lb (450 gm) potatoes, cooked and sliced
1 onion, peeled and finely chopped
seasoning
4 oz (100 gm) breadcrumbs
1½ oz (37 gm) grated strong cheese

Melt 1 oz (25 gm) butter in a frying pan until soft. Remove from the heat and stir in the eggs and cream.

Place half the potatoes in a 1-pint 'Pyrex' casserole dish and cover with onions. Pour on half the sour cream mixture. Place another layer of potatoes on this, top with onions and remaining sour cream mixture. Season to taste. Top with breadcrumbs and cover with grated cheese. Trickle remaining butter over the dish and cook uncovered, at gas mark 6, 400°F (200°C) for 30 minutes.

# Helmsley lamb

½ oz (12 gm) fat
2 lb (900 gm) neck of lamb
½ oz (12 gm) flour
1 pint (600 ml) herb stock
seasoning

1 lb (450 gm) carrots, cut into
  ½-in cubes
1 lb (450 gm) new potatoes scraped,
  cut small
8 oz (225 gm) green peas
chopped mint for garnish (optional)

Melt the fat in a heavy frying pan and brown the lamb all over in this.
Remove and place in a 2½-pint 'Pyrex' casserole. Cook the flour in the fat and
make a slightly thickened sauce by adding the stock a little at a time. Simmer
for 5 minutes, stirring constantly. Season to taste. Place the vegetables,
except the peas, round the lamb and pour over the sauce. Cover and cook
at gas mark 3, 325°F (170°C) for 1½ hours. Remove from the oven, drain
off the liquid from the casserole. Reduce it by cooking at a fast boil until the
quantity of liquid is diminished. Adjust seasoning. Pour over the meat and
vegetables and add the peas. Return to the oven for 20 minutes. Garnish
with chopped mint before serving.

# Dales rabbit casserole

1 rabbit skinned, cleaned and
  jointed
2 oz (50 gm) seasoned flour
2 oz (50 gm) fat for frying
1 onion, sliced
1 leek, sliced

1 stalk of celery, chopped
2 carrots, sliced
2 small potatoes, peeled and grated
1 pint (600 ml) herb stock
bouquet garni

Soak the rabbit joints in cold water for 1 hour. Drain and toss the joints in
the seasoned flour. Fry in the hot fat until lightly browned. Place in a 3-pint
oblong 'Pyrex' casserole dish and then fry the onion, leek, celery and carrots
for 5 minutes. Remove and place in the casserole with the grated potato. Add
the remainder of the flour to the fat and cook stirring constantly for 3
minutes. Add the herb stock slowly to the pan and simmer stirring well for
5 minutes. Add the bouquet garni and pour into the casserole. Cover and
cook at gas mark 4, 350°F (180°C) for 2 hours. Remove the bouquet garni
before serving.

large can of apricots
8 teaspoons (40 ml) of gelatine
4 tablespoons (60 ml) of cold water
4 eggs, separated

6 oz (150 gm) caster sugar
½ pint (300 ml) double cream
whipped cream
whole hazelnuts for decoration

Drain the apricots and place in a blender. Blend until the apricots form a purée. Prepare the soufflé dish by brushing a 4-in (10-cm) strip of grease-proof paper with oil: tie around the outside edge of a small 'Pyrex' soufflé dish – the paper should extend 3-in (8-cm) above the edge of the dish. Soak the gelatine in the water for 5 minutes and then pour into a saucepan. Stir over a low heat until the gelatine has dissolved. Remove from the heat and add the apricot purée.

Beat the egg yolks and sugar until light and thick. Stir in the gelatine mixture and leave until the mixture begins to set. Whisk the egg whites until stiff and beat the cream until firm; then fold the two together. Fold the gelatine and apricot mixture into this, pour into the soufflé dish and place in the refrigerator until firm.

To serve, remove the paper very carefully and decorate the top with the whipped cream and the whole hazelnuts. *Serves 6.*

# Mrs Bell's curd cheesecake

2 teaspoons (10 ml) plain flour
4 pints (2400 ml) milk – old but not sour
2 small teaspoons (7 ml) Epsom Salts
4 oz (100 gm) sugar
1 teaspoon (5 ml) golden syrup
2–3 oz (50–75 gm) butter
2 standard eggs
4 oz (100 gm) currants
rum to taste
grated peel of 1 lemon
a little candied peel (optional)
12 oz (350 gm) shortcrust pastry

Make the curd by mixing the flour with a little milk and bring the rest of the milk almost to the boil. Stir in mixed flour and milk, then Epsom Salts. Rock the pan until the milk boils and curdles and the whey clears. Leave to cool, then strain through muslin or a fine sieve. Add the sugar, syrup, butter, eggs, currants, rum, lemon peel and candied peel. Line a 2-pint 'Pyrex' Flavour Saver pie dish with the shortcrust pastry. Fill with curd mixture, allowing for pastry to rise and bake at gas mark 5, 375°F (190°C) for 35–40 minutes until curd is golden brown. *Serves 6–8.*

# The North East

*Hylton Castle*

Sunderland, in the north east, is where much of the 'Pyrex' in this book comes from. There are plenty of local recipes to draw from and some of the best cooks have recommended 'casseroled hearts' and 'rabbit and vegetable hot-pot'.

The north east is not a totally industrial area, there is a large farming community, and a local pastime is shooting, hence the 'rich farmhouse pigeon casserole' mentioned in this section!

The 'marrow and tomato casserole' is for all those keen local gardeners who grow marrows for the family to eat and to exhibit at garden shows.

# Chicken and fruit casserole

3 lb (1350 gm) chicken and giblets
1 pint (600 ml) water
1 bouquet garni
1 oz (25 gm) seasoned flour
1½ oz (37 gm) butter

1 large onion, peeled and chopped
½ lb (225 gm) dried apricots,
  previously soaked overnight
1 teaspoon (5 ml) parsley, chopped
1 dessertspoon (10 ml) honey

Cut the chicken into joints. Poach the giblets for 30–40 minutes in the water with the bouquet garni. Drain and reserve the liquor. Turn the chicken pieces in seasoned flour and fry in the hot fat with the onion until golden brown. Place in a 4¼-pint 'Pyrex' casserole and surround the chicken with the apricots. Mix the stock, parsley and honey together and heat gently. Stir the remaining flour into the fat and cook slowly for a few minutes then add the liquid a little at a time. Simmer for 15 minutes, stirring constantly. Pour over the chicken and apricots and cover the casserole dish. Cook at gas mark 4, 350°F (180°C) for 1½ hours.

# Brains and bacon

1 lb (450 gm) calves' brains
4 oz (100 gm) back bacon
½ oz (12 gm) seasoned flour
½ pint (300 ml) stock

2 tablespoons (30 ml) sherry
1 teaspoon (5 ml) Worcestershire
 sauce
chopped parsley for decoration

Soak brains in salted water for 20 minutes. Remove and place in 1½ pints (900 ml) boiling water to which you have added a pinch of salt. Reduce heat and simmer for 15 minutes. Drain well and wrap each brain in a slice of bacon. Secure with a wooden cocktail stick and place in a 2½-pint square 'Pyrex' casserole. Make a thickened sauce by mixing seasoned flour with a little stock. Heat gently in a pan adding the rest of the stock a little at a time. Stir constantly. Add the sherry and Worcestershire sauce and pour over the brains. Cover and cook at gas mark 4, 350°F (180°C) for 20 minutes. Remove from oven and decorate with chopped parsley.

# Tipsy kidneys

6 lambs kidneys
2 onions, sliced
1 oz (25 gm) fat for frying
$\frac{1}{2}$ lb (225 gm) beef sausages
$\frac{1}{2}$ oz (12 gm) flour
$\frac{1}{4}$ pint (150 ml) stock

$\frac{1}{4}$ pint (150 ml) beer
$\frac{1}{4}$ pint (150 ml) sherry
2 tablespoons (30 ml) tomato purée
seasoning
8 oz (225 gm) mushrooms

Clean and skin the kidneys, remove the core and slice the kidneys in half. Fry the onions in the fat until soft. Add the kidneys and sausages and fry for 3 minutes turning once. Remove and place in 3-pint 'Pyrex' casserole. Stir the flour into the hot fat and mix well with a wooden spoon. Add a little at a time the mixture of stock, beer, sherry and tomato purée. Season to taste and cook over a medium heat for a few minutes stirring constantly. Sprinkle the sliced mushrooms over the kidneys and pour on the sauce. Cover and cook at gas mark 4, 350°F (180°C) for 1$\frac{1}{2}$ hours.

# Northumberland casserole

$\frac{3}{4}$ lb (325 gm) lambs liver
$\frac{1}{2}$ oz (12 gm) seasoned flour
1 oz (25 gm) fat for frying
1$\frac{1}{2}$ lb (780 gm) potatoes peeled, boiled and sliced

2 large onions, sliced
6 rashers bacon
$\frac{1}{2}$ pt (300 ml) stock

Wash the liver under running water and then blanch by pouring over salted boiling water. Drain and dip into the seasoned flour coating carefully on each side. Fry quickly in hot fat. Remove from the pan and then quickly fry the potatoes and onions in the same dripping. Lay layers of liver, onions and potatoes in a 3-pint 'Pyrex' casserole. Chop the bacon rashers roughly and sprinkle over the top. Pour on stock, cover and cook at gas mark 5, 375°F (190°C) for 30 minutes.

# Casserole of celery and potatoes

1 head of celery, cleaned and trimmed
3 large potatoes
1 oz (25 gm) butter
1 small onion, finely chopped
$\frac{1}{4}$ pint (150 ml) stock
seasoning
1–2 oz (25–50 gm) thinly sliced cheese

Separate the celery stalks and cut into pieces 3-in (7.5-cm) long. Peel and slice the potatoes and cut into quarters. Grease a 2-pint 'Pyrex' casserole dish well with the butter and lay the onion, celery and potato in this. Cover with $\frac{1}{4}$ pint stock and season to taste. Cover and cook at gas mark 4, 350°F (180°C) for 20–30 minutes until potatoes are tender. Cover with thinly sliced cheese and return to oven for cheese to brown.

# Brown oxtail casserole

1 tablespoon (15 ml) dripping
3 lb (1350 gm) oxtail
6 oz (150 gm) onion, sliced
6 oz (150 gm) baby carrots
3 sticks celery, chopped

2 leeks, chopped
$\frac{1}{2}$ oz (12 gm) flour
1 pint (600 ml) stock
bouquet garni
salt and pepper

Melt the dripping in a heavy frying pan. Brown the oxtail and then the vegetables in the hot fat. Place these in a $4\frac{1}{4}$-pint 'Pyrex' casserole and add the flour to the remaining fat. Stir well and add the stock a little at a time, stirring constantly. Add bouquet garni and seasoning and simmer for 5 minutes. Pour over meat and vegetables and cook at gas mark 4, 350°F (180°C) for 4 hours. Remove bouquet garni before serving.

4 lambs hearts, thawed
½ pint (300 ml) stock

1 glass sweet sherry

**Stuffing**
2 oz (50 gm) cooked ham, diced
4 oz (100 gm) fresh breadcrumbs
1 tablespoon (15 ml) parsley,
   chopped

pinch of sage, rosemary, thyme
salt and pepper
1 egg, beaten
juice of half a lemon

Trim the excess fat from the hearts and cut the dividing wall to make a cavity. Soak for 1 hour in cold water. Rinse well and drain. Mix the dry ingredients together and bind with egg and lemon juice. Pack the stuffing well into the hearts. Place in a 2½-pint oval 'Pyrex' casserole, pour over the stock and cover with a tight-fitting lid. Baste the hearts frequently, while cooking. Cook for 1½ hours at gas Mark 3, 325°F (170°C). In the last half-hour of cooking add the sherry.

  Serve piping hot with a selection of vegetables.

# Cidered haddock casserole

1–1½ lb (450–700 gm) haddock or cod fillet, skinned
½ lb (225 gm) tomatoes, skinned and sliced
2 oz (50 gm) button mushrooms, sliced
1 tablespoon (15 ml) parsley, chopped

salt and freshly ground black pepper
¼ pint (150 ml) cider
2 tablespoons (30 ml) fresh white breadcrumbs
2 tablespoons (30 ml) cheese, grated

Wipe the fish, cut into cubes and lay these in a 3-pint 'Pyrex' oblong casserole. Cover with the sliced tomatoes and mushrooms, the parsley and seasoning and pour the cider over. Cover with lid and cook in the centre of the oven at gas mark 4, 350°F (180°C) for 20–25 minutes. Sprinkle with the breadcrumbs and cheese and brown in a hot oven, gas mark 7, 425°F (220°C) or under a hot grill.

# Gamekeeper's rabbit casserole

4 large rabbit joints
1 onion
1 tablespoon (15 ml) oil
$\frac{1}{2}$ oz (12 gm) butter
2 oz (50 gm) tomato purée
2 sticks celery

1 tablespoon (15 ml) capers
1 tablespoon (15 ml) sugar
$\frac{1}{4}$ pint (150 ml) red wine
$\frac{1}{2}$ pint (300 ml) stock
thyme, salt, pepper
$\frac{1}{2}$ oz (12 gm) cornflour

Wash and dry the rabbit pieces and place in a $4\frac{1}{4}$-pint 'Pyrex' casserole. Fry the onion in the oil together with butter until brown and add to the casserole together with the tomato purée, chopped celery, capers, sugar, red wine, stock and seasoning. Stir the ingredients well, cover and cook for $1\frac{1}{2}$ hours at gas mark 4, 350°F (180°C) until the rabbit is tender. Blend the cornflour in a little water and stir into the casserole mixture. Return to the oven for 15 minutes.

# Rich farmhouse pigeon casserole

2 pigeons
1 oz (25 gm) butter
8 oz (225 gm) stewing steak
1 rasher of bacon
$\frac{1}{2}$ pint (300 ml) stock
2 oz (50 gm) mushrooms

salt, pepper
1 tablespoon (15 ml) lemon juice
1 tablespoon (15 ml)
   redcurrant jelly
$\frac{1}{2}$ oz (12 gm) plain flour
a little water

Cut the pigeons in half and fry in butter until browned. Cut the steak into cubes and dice the bacon. Place all three meats in a $4\frac{1}{2}$-pint 'Pyrex' oval casserole and cover with stock, mushrooms and seasoning. Cover and cook for 2 hours at gas mark 4, 350°F (180°c). Then mix together the lemon juice, redcurrant jelly, flour and a little water and stir into the casserole. Return to the oven and cook for a further 15 minutes.

# Pork and prune casserole

2 oz (50 gm) prunes
1 lb (450 gm) lean pork, boned
1 lb (450 gm) potatoes
$\frac{1}{2}$ lb (225 gm) onions

salt, pepper
$\frac{1}{4}$ pint (150 ml) stock
1 packet sage and onion stuffing
1 large, red–skinned eating apple

Soak the prunes overnight then cut in half and remove the stones. Cut the pork into cubes and place in a 3-pint 'Pyrex' round casserole with the prunes and the peeled and sliced potatoes and onions. Season and add the stock. Cover and cook slowly for $1\frac{1}{2}$ hours at gas mark 3, 325°F (180°C) until the meat is tender. Meanwhile prepare the stuffing mixture and form into small balls. Core and slice the apple. When the casserole is cooked add the stuffing balls and arrange the apple slices around the edge. Place in the oven until the apples are browned.

4¼ oz (105 gm) sugar
6 tablespoons (90 ml) water
1 teaspoon (5 ml) lemon juice

18 oz tin (500 gm) raspberries
and blackberries
8 slices of bread

Melt sugar in water over a low heat and bring slowly to the boil. Add the fruit and lemon juice and stir well. Remove the crusts from the bread and cut into wide strips. Place a circle of bread in the base of a 2-pint 'Pyrex' pudding basin and pack the strips around the sides (use a wedge-shape piece of bread to fill in any gaps). Pour in the fruit mixture and cut more strips or a large circle to cover fruit. Place a saucer and a weight on top and leave in a cool place overnight. Turn out the pudding and serve with fresh whipped cream. *Serves 6.*

# Peaches and cream pie

6 oz (150 gm) shortcrust pastry
large tin of peach halves
1 tablespoon (15 ml) sherry
$\frac{1}{2}$ teaspoon (2.5 ml) cinnamon
2 oz (50 gm) fresh white
  breadcrumbs

1 tablespoon (15 ml) lemon juice
1 oz (25 gm) butter, melted
double cream for decoration

Roll out the pastry and line an $8\frac{1}{2}$-inch 'Pyrex' pie plate. Bake blind for 20 minutes at gas mark 7, 425°F (220°C). Remove from the oven and leave to cool. Meanwhile, mix a little of the juice from the canned peaches with the sherry and cinnamon. Mix the breadcrumbs into this and spread over the base of the pastry case. Place the peach halves on the breadcrumbs and pour some more juice mixed with the lemon juice and melted butter over the peaches just to moisten them. Place in the oven and bake at gas mark 4, 350°F (180°C) for 25 minutes. When completely cold, beat the double cream and pipe over the pie. Serve immediately. *Serves 6.*

# The North West

*Watendtlath*

Those of us who don't live in this beautiful area of Britain tend to think of it only in terms of annual holidays.

'Individual casseroles' have been devised from a mammoth sausage casserole we sampled on a working trip in the Lake District and the 'grape and pigeon casserole' will grace any dinner party, as will 'hot chocolate soufflé'–very nice served with a local fudge sauce.

# Westmorland bean hot pot

1 lb (450 gm) butter beans
8 oz (225 gm) bacon rashers
1 oz (25 gm) demerara sugar

1 tablespoon (15 ml) syrup
1 teaspoon (15 ml) mustard
¾ pint (450 ml) boiling water

Soak the beans in cold water overnight. Rinse then place in a 3-pint round 'Pyrex' casserole with the bacon. Mix the sugar, syrup and mustard with the boiling water and pour over the beans. Cover and bake at gas mark 3, 325°F (170°C) for 3 hours.

# Lakeland hot pot

1 lb (450 gm) lamb's liver
2 large onions
¼ lb (100 gm) lean bacon
1 oz (25 gm) flour

2 oz (50 gm) butter
½ pint (300 ml) herb stock
salt and pepper
1 lb (450 gm) potatoes

Slice the liver and onions and chop the bacon. Coat the liver in the flour and fry in the butter very gently with the bacon and onions. Stir in stock and season to taste. Transfer into a 2½-pint oval 'Pyrex' casserole and arrange the sliced potatoes around the edge. Cover and bake for 1½ hours at gas mark 4, 350°F (180°C). Remove lid during last half hour of cooking in order to brown the potatoes.

# Individual sausage casseroles

4 pork sausages, cooked, cold
6 beaten eggs
2 10 oz (275 gm) cans sweetcorn

4 tablespoons (60 ml) melted butter
salt and pepper
4 stuffed olives

Butter four individual 8-oz round 'Pyrex' casserole dishes. Slice the sausages and arrange equally on the base of each dish. Mix together the remaining ingredients, except the olives, and pour over the sausages in the casseroles. Bake at gas mark 3, 325°F (170°C) for 30–40 minutes, until the mixture is firm. Garnish each with sliced, stuffed olives.

# Grape and pigeon casserole

4 pigeons
2 tablespoons (30 ml) oil
8 rashers bacon
1 onion, chopped
4 tablespoons (60 ml)
  redcurrant jelly

$\frac{1}{2}$ pint (300 ml) stock
$\frac{1}{2}$ teaspoon (2.5 ml) nutmeg, grated
salt and pepper
8 oz (225 gm) green or black grapes

Prepare and clean the pigeons. Heat the oil in a frying pan and fry four of the bacon rashers, chopped, together with the onion, for 5 minutes. Remove and place in $4\frac{1}{4}$-pint 'Pyrex' casserole. Wrap each pigeon with the remaining rashers of bacon and fry in the pan until browned. Add to the casserole. Place the jelly, stock, nutmeg and seasoning in the pan and just bring to the boil. Pour over the pigeons and cook for 3 hours at gas mark 3, 325°F (170°C). Add the grapes and put back in the oven for 5 more minutes.

# Lancashire tripe casserole

1 lb (450 gm) tripe
1 oz (25 gm) fat
1 oz (25 gm) flour
$\frac{1}{4}$ pint (150 ml) beef stock
$\frac{1}{4}$ teaspoon (1.2 ml) ground ginger
$\frac{1}{4}$ teaspoon (1.2 ml) ground nutmeg
celery salt

pepper
2 onions, peeled and sliced
2 carrots, sliced
1 turnip, peeled and chopped
2 oz (50 gm) Lancashire cheese,
   grated

Clean the tripe and cut into 2-in (5-cm) pieces. Melt fat in a frying pan, stir in the flour and gradually add the stock. Bring to the boil and simmer for a few minutes. Add the spices and seasonings and stir well. Then add the prepared vegetables and simmer for a further 3 minutes. Add the pieces of tripe and mix into the gravy and vegetable mixture. Transfer into a 3-pint round 'Pyrex' casserole, cover and cook for $2\frac{1}{2}$ hours, at gas mark 2, 300°F (150°C) until the tripe is tender. Sprinkle the grated cheese on top just before serving.

# Farmer's hot pot

4 mutton chops
1 oz (25 gm) flour
salt and pepper
1 oz (25 gm) fat for frying
4 large onions

6 carrots
6 large potatoes
$\frac{3}{4}$ pint (450 ml) water
1 dessertspoon (10 ml) brown sugar

Coat the chops in flour and seasoning and fry for a few minutes in the fat. Place in a 3-pint round 'Pyrex' casserole. Chop the onions and carrots and fry until slightly browned. Add to the chops. Cut the potatoes into thick slices and arrange on top, adding seasoning. Stir the remaining flour into the fat in which the chops and vegetables have been fried and add the water to make a thick gravy. Add the sugar. Pour this over the potatoes. Cover and cook for 2 hours at gas mark 4, 350°F (180°C). Remove the lid for the last half-hour to brown the potatoes.

# Hot chocolate soufflé

2½ oz (70 gm) butter
1½ oz (37 gm) flour
½ pint (300 ml) milk, warm

3½ oz (88 gm) plain chocolate
2½ oz (70 gm) sugar
4 eggs, separated

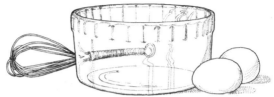

Melt the butter in a saucepan and blend in the flour, cook slowly for about a minute. Remove from heat and gradually stir in the warm milk, heating slowly until a smooth sauce is formed. Melt the chocolate in a small bowl over a saucepan of hot water and then stir into the sauce together with the sugar. Beat in the egg yolks. Whisk the whites until stiff and fold into the mixture very thoroughly. Butter a small 'Pyrex' soufflé dish and pour in the mixture. Stand the dish in a shallow pan of hot water and bake at gas mark 6, 400°F (200°C) for about 30 minutes until the soufflé is well risen and browned. *Serves 6.*

# Mincemeat flan

4 oz (100 gm) butter
8 oz (225 gm) digestive biscuits
1 jar mincemeat
1 tablespoon (15 ml) brandy

1 small can pineapple pieces,
  drained
2 egg yolks, beaten
2 egg whites
4 oz (100 gm) caster sugar

Melt the butter in a pan, crush the biscuits with a rolling pin and add them
to the butter. Mix well and press over the base and sides of a 1¾-pint
'Pyrex' flan dish. Place in the refrigerator until firm. Mix the mincemeat,
brandy and pineapple together in a saucepan. Add the egg yolks and stir
over a low heat for a few minutes. Turn the mixture into the flan dish,
allow to cool and refrigerate for 1 hour. Whisk the egg whites until stiff,
add half the sugar and whisk again until stiff. Add the remainder of the
sugar and fold in gently. Pipe the meringue in a lattice over the mincemeat
and around the edge of the crumb crust. Bake at gas mark 7, 425°F (220°C)
for 5 minutes. Serve cold.

# Wales

*Harlech Castle*

Some of the most beautiful parts of Britain are to be seen along the coast of Wales and the border area; locating recipes was a delightful job and sampling the foods put on the pounds!

Lamb is quite a popular food and the 'Brecon hot pot' is a good example of superb Welsh cookery. Follow this with 'blackcurrant stuffed pancakes' and wait for compliments.

# Leek and sherry casserole

1 oz (25 gm) butter
2 rashers bacon, chopped
1 carrot, sliced
1 celery stalk, chopped
4 large leeks, washed and trimmed

$\frac{1}{2}$ teaspoon (2·5 ml) salt
$\frac{1}{4}$ teaspoon (1.2 ml) sage
$1\frac{1}{4}$ fl oz (40 ml) sherry
$\frac{1}{4}$ pint (150 ml) stock
$1\frac{1}{4}$ fl oz (40 ml) cream

Melt the butter in a frying pan and fry the bacon, carrot and celery until golden. Slice leeks lengthways and lay in a lightly greased $2\frac{1}{2}$-pint 'Pyrex' casserole dish, cover with the bacon and vegetables. Add the salt, sage and sherry to the stock and pour over the leeks. Trickle the cream over the top, cover and place in the oven. Cook at gas mark 4, 350°F (180°C) for 45 minutes.

| | |
|---|---|
| 1 small marrow | salt and pepper |
| 1 small onion, chopped | 2 fl oz (60 ml) milk |
| 1 oz (25 gm) butter or margarine | little nutmeg, grated |
| 2 oz (50 gm) cheese, grated | $\frac{3}{4}$ oz (20 gm) fine dried breadcrumbs |

Pre-heat oven to hot, gas mark 6, 400°F (200°C). Prepare marrow as for boiling. Cook in boiling salted water for 7 minutes. Drain. Rub the inside of a 1-pint 'Pyrex' casserole dish with chopped onion. Melt $\frac{1}{2}$ oz (12 gm) butter and use to brush inside of dish. Fill with layers of marrow and most of the grated cheese, sprinkling salt and pepper between layers. Pour milk into dish, then dot top with flakes of the remaining butter and the cheese. Sprinkle lightly with nutmeg followed by crumbs. Bake near top of oven for 15 to 20 minutes.

Serve with meat roasts, grills and fish dishes.

# Kidney and sausage hot pot

1½ lb (700 gm) ox kidney
½ lb (225 gm) pork sausages
½ oz (12 gm) flour
2 oz (50 gm) fat
2 carrots

1 onion
½ pint (300 ml) stock
4 oz (100 gm) button mushrooms
salt, pepper
parsley, chopped

Prepare the kidney by removing the skin and cutting out the core from the middle. Wash and dry and cut into pieces. Cut the sausages into threes and coat these and the kidney with the flour. Fry both meats in the fat for a few minutes. Remove and fry the sliced carrots and onion until slightly browned. Add the stock and bring to the boil. Pour this into a 3-pint 'Pyrex' casserole, add the meat, mushrooms and seasoning and cook for 2 hours at gas mark 3, 325°F (170°C). Sprinkle with chopped parsley before serving.

# Brecon hot pot

4 lambs' kidneys
4 lean lamb chops 1-in (2.5-cm)
  thick
1 oz (25 gm) butter
4 potatoes, peeled and sliced

fresh black pepper, salt
8 oz (225 gm) fresh mushrooms
2 onions, peeled and chopped
¾ pint (450 ml) water
parsley, chopped

Trim the fat from the kidneys and lamb chops. Grease a 2-pint round 'Pyrex' casserole with half the butter and arrange one third of the sliced potatoes on the bottom. Place two of the chops on top and sprinkle with salt and pepper. Add half the kidneys, half the mushrooms and half the onions and cover with another third of the potatoes. Place the other chops on top and season. Add the remaining kidneys, mushrooms and onions and arrange the potatoes evenly on top. Pour in the water. Dot with the remainder of the butter, cover and cook at gas mark 4, 350°F (180°C) for 1½ hours. Remove lid and cook for a further 30 minutes until the top is brown. Sprinkle with parsley.

# New year pheasant

2 pheasants, jointed
1 oz (25 gm) dripping
mixture of chopped:
  ½ lb (225 gm) swedes
  ½ lb (225 gm) turnips
  ½ lb (225 gm) parsnips
  ½ lb (225 gm) carrots

½ lb (225 gm) onions
seasoning
1 oz (25 gm) flour
large wineglass of sherry
½ pint (300 ml) pouring cream
½ lb (225 gm) tomatoes
bouquet garni

Fry the pheasant pieces in the hot dripping. Remove and place in a 5-pint 'Pyrex' casserole. Fry the chopped vegetables except the tomatoes, adding seasoning. Drain and arrange these over and around the pheasant, add flour to fat and cook slowly. Mix the sherry and cream together and stir into the flour mixture. Add a little stock if necessary. Heat gently for 5 minutes, stirring continuously. Pour over pheasant, add the tomatoes and bouquet garni and cook at gas mark 4, 350°F (180°C) for 1 hour.

2 oz (50 gm) butter
1 small leek, chopped (green part only)
2 oz (50 gm) flour
8 oz (225 ml) chicken stock
½ pint (300 ml) single cream
wineglass of sherry
1 teaspoon (5 ml) Worcestershire sauce

seasoning plus pinch of red pepper
1 teaspoon (5 ml) sugar
12 oz (350 gm) cooked chicken, pulled into pieces
6 oz (170 gm) cooked rice
4 oz (100 gm) sliced mushrooms
2 tablespoons (30 ml) parsley, chopped

Melt the butter, add the chopped leek and fry for 1 minute. Stir in the flour, add the stock and cream and cook slowly, stirring constantly, until mixture is thick and smooth. Add sherry, Worcestershire sauce, seasonings, and sugar. Stir and remove from heat. Place the chicken and rice in a 3-pint oblong 'Pyrex' casserole and pour over the sauce. Place the mushrooms on top and cover. Cook at gas mark 4, 350°F (180°C) for 45 minutes. Garnish with chopped parsley.

# Crusty lamb casserole

2 lb (900 gm) breast or shoulder of lamb
1 oz (25 gm) seasoned flour
1 oz (25 gm) fat for frying
2 onions, sliced

$\frac{1}{2}$ head of celery, chopped
1 pint (600 ml) herb stock
2 tablespoons (30 ml) tomato purée
$\frac{1}{4}$ teaspoon (0.6 ml) salt
4 small buttered slices of bread

Cut the meat into cubes and turn in seasoned flour. Heat the fat in a frying pan, add the vegetables and fry until light golden. Move to one side of the pan and sear the meat in the hot fat. Transfer meat and vegetables to a 3-pint 'Pyrex' casserole and add the herb stock into which you have stirred the tomato purée and salt. Cover and cook at gas mark 3, 325°F (170°C) for 2 hours. Remove from the oven. Cut each slice of bread in half and place around the sides of the dish. Return to the oven, without the casserole lid, for 20–30 minutes until the bread is golden brown.

# Ruthin potted pork

¾ lb (350 gm) lean boneless pork, cut into ½-in (1-cm) cubes
4 oz (110 gm) fresh pork fat, cut into ¼-in (0.5-cm) cubes
½ teaspoon (1.2 ml) salt
freshly ground black pepper
3¾ fl oz (115 ml) of water
1 large bay leaf
2 whole cloves

Preheat oven to gas mark ½, 250°F (130°C). Toss together pork, pork fat, salt and a few grindings of pepper in a 2-pint round 'Pyrex' casserole. Pour in the water, add the bay leaf and cloves, and cover tightly. Bake in the centre of the oven for about 4 hours, until most of the liquid has evaporated and the pork is tender enough to be mashed against the side of the casserole with a spoon. Do not let the pork brown. Check the casserole occasionally and, if the liquid seems to be cooking away, add more water a tablespoon or so at a time.

Transfer the pork to a shallow bowl with a perforated spoon. Discard the bay leaf and cloves, and reserve all the fat and cooking juices. Cut away any bits of gristle and shred the pork as finely as possible with a fork. Stir in the reserved fat and juices, then pack the mixture tightly into a 1 lb (450 gm) stone jar, a terrine or an earthenware crock. Cover with a lid or foil, allow to cool and refrigerate for at least 24 hours before serving. Potted pork is traditionally served with hot toast as a first course or at teatime.

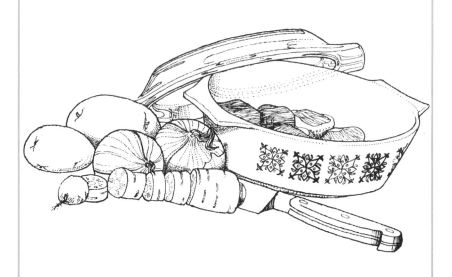

# Blackcurrant stuffed pancakes

4 oz (100 gm) plain flour
pinch of salt
1 egg
$\frac{1}{4}$ pint (150 ml) milk
$\frac{1}{4}$ pint (150 ml) water

1 tablespoon (15 ml) oil
$\frac{1}{2}$ oz (12 gm) lard
1 large tin blackcurrant pie filling
  (or jar of blackcurrant jam)
$\frac{1}{2}$ pint (300 ml) thin cream

Make the pancake batter by sifting the flour and salt into a 'Pyrex' mixing bowl. Hollow out the centre, and break the egg into the hole. Add a little of the milk. Stir gradually, drawing in the flour from the sides of the bowl, until the mixture thickens. Add the rest of the milk a little at a time until the batter is smooth. Stir in the water and oil and beat for 1 minute. Leave to stand for 1 hour.

Make about 9 or 10 very thin pancakes by melting a little lard in a frying pan and pouring in about 2 tablespoons (30 ml) of the mixture to coat the pan. Cook quickly on both sides. Pile on to a plate and keep warm. Spread each pancake with a little of the blackcurrant filling and roll up. Place in a 'Pyrex' general purpose dish and pour the cream over the top. Heat through for about 15 minutes at gas mark 4, 350°F (180°C). *Serves 6.*

6 oz (150 gm) self-raising flour
½ teaspoon (1.2 ml) ginger
8 oz (225 gm) butter
6 oz (150 gm) caster sugar
1½ oz (40 gm) flaked nuts

1 lb 13 oz (822 gm) can apricot
  halves
2 oz (50 gm) Barbados sugar
1 oz (25 gm) butter
3 eggs

Sieve the flour and ginger. Cream the butter and caster sugar until light and fluffy. Gradually beat in the eggs, and then fold in the sieved flour and ginger. Grease a 'Pyrex' Flavour Saver and fill with the creamed mixture. Press half the drained apricot halves into the mixture. Spoon over 2 tablespoons of the apricot juice and sprinkle with half the Barbados sugar. Bake at gas mark 4, 350°F (180°C) for 45 minutes. Top with the remaining drained apricot halves, melted butter and scatter with the remaining Barbados sugar and the nuts. Serve warm. *Serves 6.*

# The Border Country

*Hadrian's Wall*

The border country is the area around Hadrian's Wall – that line that runs along the Cheviot Hills through Tweed, Teviotdale Liddesdale and Gretna.

Many of the recipes are drawn from local sources. Game, salmon, trout and sea–fish appear in local dishes. Certainly other foods are used in abundance and a particular favourite is 'Ettrick lamb in cider'. 'Hot creamy herrings' are nice too, particularly on a cold winter's day, for luncheon or supper.

# Trout in white wine

4 trout, cleaned
salt and pepper
1 onion, finely chopped
2 oz (50 gm) butter
8 oz (225 gm) mushrooms,
  finely chopped

1 tablespoon (15 ml) parsley,
  chopped
1 tablespoon (15 ml) of lemon juice
$\frac{1}{4}$ pint (150 ml) dry white wine

Clean the trout thoroughly. Split and bone carefully. Season inside and out. Fry the onion in the butter until soft and add the mushrooms, parsley and lemon juice. Put this mixture inside each fish and place the fish in a 3-pint 'Pyrex' casserole. Cover with wine and cook at gas mark 5, 375°F (190°C) for 30 minutes.

# Chestnut and partridge casserole

1 oz (25 gm) butter
2 partridges
2 oz (50 gm) bacon
8 oz (225 gm) chestnuts, peeled

1 apple, sliced
seasoning
1 wineglass red wine
$\frac{1}{4}$ pint (150 ml) stock

Melt the butter and brown the partridges. Dice the bacon and place in the bottom of a 3-pint oblong 'Pyrex' casserole with the partridges, add the chestnuts, apple, seasoning, red wine and stock. Pour over the butter remaining after browning the partridges and cook at gas mark 3, 325°F (170°C) for $1\frac{1}{2}$ hours.

# Hot creamy herrings

4 large herrings
1 tablespoon (15 ml) English
  mustard
2 teaspoons (10 ml) milk
1 tablespoon (15 ml) tomato purée

1 teaspoon (5 ml) brown sugar
seasoning
1 lemon
parsley, finely chopped
2 tablespoons (30 ml) cream

Clean the herrings thoroughly and fillet using the flat side of a sharp
pointed knife. Mix the mustard and milk together to make a creamy mixture,
then add this to the cream, tomato purée and brown sugar. Season to taste.
Grate the rind of the lemon and add a pinch of this to the cream mixture.
Lay each herring flat. Spread mixture on each fish and roll herrings up from
tail end. Fit tightly into a 2-pint 'Pyrex' casserole dish and squeeze the juice
of the lemon over these. Cover and cook at gas mark 4, 350°F (180°C) for
30 minutes. Remove lid and sprinkle on chopped parsley before serving.

# Border country salmon in cream

4 fresh salmon steaks 1 in (2.5 cm)
  thick
salt
$\frac{1}{2}$ pint (300 ml) fresh or sour cream
1 tablespoon (15 ml) lemon juice

1 tablespoon (15 ml) dill leaves,
  finely chopped
1–2 tablespoons (15 –30 ml)
  French mustard
parsley, chopped

Sprinkle the salmon steaks with salt and place in a 3-pint oblong 'Pyrex'
casserole. Mix the cream, lemon juice, dill leaves and mustard together and
pour over the steaks. Cook in a moderate oven, gas mark 4, 350°F (180°C),
for about 30 minutes. Garnish with chopped parsley.

# Ettrick lamb and cider

2 lb (900 gm) of boned leg of lamb
1 oz (25 gm) flour
1 oz (25 gm) fat for frying
2 onions
3 tablespoons (45 ml) parsley,
  chopped

$\frac{1}{4}$ pint (150 ml) stock
$\frac{1}{4}$ pint (150 ml) sharp cider
1 teaspoon (5 ml) salt
$\frac{3}{4}$ fl oz (24 ml) Worcestershire sauce
1 teaspoon (5ml) pepper

Cut the meat into cubes and turn in the flour. Heat the fat and fry the meat
and onions in this. Turn into a 2½-pint oval 'Pyrex' casserole and sprinkle
on 2 tablespoons parsley. Add the stock and cider to the frying pan and stir
until boiling. Add Worcestershire sauce and seasonings and simmer for 5
minutes. Pour over the meat and cover. Cook at gas mark 3, 325°F (170°C)
for 1½ hours. Sprinkle with remaining parsley before serving.

# Winter sun casserole

2½ fl oz (65 ml) Worcestershire sauce
½ pint (300 ml) plus 4 tablespoons (60 ml) water
1 teaspoon (5 ml) salt
1 teaspoon (5 ml) pepper
1½ lb (700 gm) shin of beef, cut into cubes
1 oz (25 gm) dripping
4 large carrots, sliced
2 leeks, sliced
8 oz (225 gm) swede, cut into cubes
2 oz (50 gm) flour
½ pint (300 ml) brown ale
15 oz (425 gm) can butter beans, drained

Mix together the Worcestershire sauce, 4 tablespoons (60 ml) of the water and the salt. Put the beef cubes in a shallow dish. Pour over the Worcestershire sauce mixture and leave to marinate in the refrigerator for 4 hours, or overnight, turning occasionally. Drain meat and reserve the marinade. Heat the dripping in a frying pan and brown the meat on all sides. Remove from the pan with a slotted spoon and place in a 2½-pint oval 'Pyrex' casserole. Add all the vegetables, except the beans, to the frying pan and cook gently for 5 minutes. Blend in the flour. Remove from the heat and gradually stir in the remaining water, the ale, reserved marinade and pepper. Return to the heat and bring to the boil, stirring. Pour into the casserole, stir, cover and cook in a warm oven, gas mark 3, 325°F (170°C) for 2 hours. Add the butter beans and cook for a further 1 hour. Taste and adjust the seasoning before serving.

# Pheasant and walnut casserole

1 pheasant
1½ oz (37 gm) butter
4 rashers of bacon
rind and juice of two large oranges
wineglass of port

wineglass of stock
seasoning
1 head of celery
3 oz (75 gm) shelled chopped
  walnuts

Peel the oranges thinly and squeeze the juice. Brown the pheasant in 1 oz (25 gm) of the butter.

Lard the pheasant with the rashers of bacon and place in the base of a 5-pint 'Pyrex' casserole. Add orange juice and port, seasoning and stock. Cook at gas mark 4, 350°F (180°C) for 45 minutes. Trim the celery and slice. Fry the walnuts and celery, keeping the celery crisp. Shred the orange rind, plunge into boiling water and then stand for 1 minute in cold water. Add the celery and walnuts to the casserole and cook for a further 15 minutes. Remove 2 rashers of bacon and put the pheasant and its garnish into the lid of the casserole and scatter the orange peel over the top.

# St Abbs casserole

1½ lb (700 gm) cod or haddock
1 lemon
seasoning
4 oz (100 gm) mushrooms,
  chopped finely
1 onion, chopped finely
2 leeks, well washed and thickly
  sliced

8 oz (225 gm) tomatoes skinned and
  chopped *or*
8 oz (225 gm) can tomatoes, drained
1 tablespoon (15 ml) Barbados sugar
1 oz (25 gm) butter

Divide fish into manageable portions and place in a buttered 3-pint 'Pyrex'
casserole. Squeeze the juice of the lemon and grate the rind finely over the
fish. Season well.

Add the vegetables to the dish, scatter the brown sugar over the top and
dot with pieces of butter. Cook at gas mark 3, 325°F (170°C) for 45 minutes.

# Veal casserole

2 lb (900 gm) stewing veal
1 oz (25 gm) plain flour
seasoning
1½ oz (37 gm) fat for frying
3 onions, peeled and sliced
1 lb (450 gm) green beans

2 sticks celery, chopped
1 lb (450 gm) tomatoes, skinned
  and sliced
1 lb (450 gm) new carrots, scraped
½ pint (300 ml) herb stock

Turn the meat in the seasoned flour. Melt the fat and brown the veal quickly.
Add the onions, beans and celery. Place in a 4¼-pint 'Pyrex' casserole. Add
tomatoes and carrots to the casserole. Stir the remaining flour into the fat
and cook until golden. Gradually add the stock, stirring constantly. Bring
to the boil and simmer for a few minutes until the sauce thickens slightly.
Pour over the meat and vegetables. Cook at gas mark 3, 325°F (170°C) for
1½ hours.

# Cooking apple cake

12 oz (350 gm) shortcrust pastry
2 oz (50 gm) fresh brown
  breadcrumbs
4 large cooking apples, peeled and
  sliced

2 oz (50 gm) mixed fruit
½ teaspoon (2.5 ml) mixed spice
2 oz (50 gm) caster sugar
2 oz (50 gm) syrup
juice of 1 lemon

Line a 1¾-pint 'Pyrex' flan dish with half the pastry. Place the breadcrumbs in the bottom of the dish. Put the apple on top of the breadcrumbs and cover with the remainder of the ingredients. Cover with the pastry remaining and bake at gas mark 4, 350°F (180°C) for 40 minutes. Serve with cream or pouring custard. *Serves 6.*

# Olde English lemon mould

½ oz (12 gm) gelatine
1 pint (600 ml) milk
⅛ pint (75 ml) single cream

2½ oz (62 gm) granulated sugar
1 lemon

Sprinkle the gelatine into ¼ pint (150 ml) of milk. Pour the remaining milk, cream and sugar into a saucepan and warm gently, stirring until the sugar has dissolved. Bring to simmering heat but do not boil. Add the lemon rind. Pour in the milk and gelatine and the juice of the lemon. Stir and pour into a 1-pint 'Pyrex' jelly mould. Leave to set and turn out on to a flat plate to serve.

# Scotland

*Loch Lomond*

There is a wide variety of dishes from Scotland in this section. Tastes in food and methods of preparation vary considerably all over Scotland. There is plenty of salmon 'poached' or bought, and, in the right season from the right people, game of all varieties.

'Corn and haddock casserole' was a favourite meal on visits to the north and 'blushing rice pudding' is a simple way of producing a very cheap and attractive sweet—a favourite with children and adults alike.

# Corn and haddock casserole

2 medium potatoes
1 lb (450 gm) haddock fillets
2 oz (50 gm) melted butter
seasoning

8 oz (225 gm) can sweetcorn
1 tablespoon (15 ml) parsley,
chopped

Peel and boil the potatoes and drain them. Put to one side and allow to cool. Cut the fish into eight pieces. Brush the fish with melted butter and season with salt and pepper. Sprinkle chopped parsley on each piece of fish and roll up tightly. Secure with a wooden cocktail stick. Pack tightly in a 2-pint 'Pyrex' casserole dish. Slice the boiled potatoes thickly and arrange around the edges of the dish. Pour the sweetcorn from the can in the space between the fish and potatoes. Brush the fish and potatoes with the remaining melted butter and cover. Cook at gas mark 6, 400°F (200°C) for 30 minutes.

# Affric partridge casserole

8 oz (225 gm) streaky bacon
3 partridges and seasoning
8 oz (225 gm) little whole onions
8 oz (225 gm) whole button
   mushrooms (reserve trimmings)
$\frac{1}{4}$ pint (150 ml) red wine
$1\frac{1}{2}$ pints (900 ml) stock

bouquet garni
1 oz (25 gm) vegetable fat
1 small onion, finely chopped
$\frac{1}{2}$ oz (12 gm) flour
1 tablespoon (15 ml) parsley,
   chopped

Dice bacon, reserving half. Heat remainder in heavy saucepan until fat runs, add partridges. Brown all over. Place in a 5-pint 'Pyrex' casserole and add whole onions and whole mushrooms. Pour over red wine and $\frac{1}{2}$ pint (300 ml) of the stock and add bouquet garni. Place in centre of moderately slow oven, gas mark 3, 325°F (170°C) for 2–2$\frac{1}{2}$ hours.

Meanwhile heat remaining pieces of bacon in saucepan in vegetable fat. Add onion and cook gently until soft. Add flour, continue to cook gently until roux is dark brown colour (15 minutes). Stir in remaining stock, bring to boil, stirring. Add mushroom trimmings. Simmer for 30 minutes, thinning with stock if necessary. When partridge is cooked, remove from casserole and strain liquid off into sauce. Cut birds in half, remove breast and leg section from carcass. Replace these in casserole. Pour seasoned sauce over birds. Sprinkle with parsley and serve.

# Venison in beer

1 pint (600 ml) beer
8 oz (225 gm) brown sugar
2 tablespoons (30 ml) black treacle

3 lb (1350 gm) hung stewing
   venison

Heat the beer in a saucepan and dissolve the sugar and treacle in this over a low heat. Cut the venison into serving-size pieces and place in a $4\frac{1}{4}$-pint 'Pyrex' casserole. Cover with the beer mixture and cook at gas mark 4, 350°F (180°C) for 2 hours.

Serve with seasonal vegetables.

# Beef and bacon casserole

2 oz (50 gm) bacon
1 lb (450 gm) small potatoes
1½ lb (700 gm) stewing steak
1 oz (25 gm) fat for frying
2 large onions, sliced

1 oz (25 gm) flour
salt and pepper
1 sprig thyme
1 bay leaf
1 pint (600 ml) beef stock

Chop the bacon and fry, peel the potatoes and cut into cubes. Cut the stewing steak into even pieces and sear in the hot fat. Remove from pan and fry the onions until soft. Add flour, herbs and seasonings and beef stock a little at a time. Place the meat in a 3-pint 'Pyrex' casserole with potatoes and onions and cover with beef stock. Cook at gas mark 3, 325°F (170°C) for 2 hours.

Serve with green beans and buttered carrots.

# Minty trout

4 rainbow trout
salt and pepper
4 sprigs of fresh mint
2 oz (50 gm) butter

2 lemons
2–3 teaspoons (10–15 ml) fresh mint,
  finely chopped

Preheat oven to moderately hot, gas mark 5, 375°F (190°C).

Trim tail and remove fins from trout. Season the inside of each fish with salt and pepper and insert a sprig of mint. Arrange trout in a 2½-pint oval 'Pyrex' casserole, dot with butter and sprinkle with juice of one lemon. Cover closely with lid or foil and cook in centre of oven for 20–30 minutes, or until fish is cooked through. Sprinkle with freshly chopped mint and garnish with slices of lemon.

# Sliced Angus beef
## with wine

4 1-in (2.5-cm) thick slices of
  topside
$\frac{1}{4}$ pint (150 ml) red wine
1 onion, chopped
1 bay leaf
1 teaspoon (5 ml) parsley
$\frac{1}{2}$ teaspoon (2.5 ml) thyme
1 sprig marjoram

1 oz (25 gm) dripping
1 oz (25 gm) flour
$\frac{1}{2}$ pint (300 ml) beef stock
$\frac{1}{2}$ lb (225 gm) carrots, sliced
$\frac{1}{2}$ lb (225 gm) tiny onions
seasoning
1 tablespoon (15 ml) parsley,
  chopped

Marinate the beef by laying it in a $2\frac{1}{2}$-pint 'Pyrex' general purpose dish and pouring over this the red wine, chopped onion and the herbs. Leave overnight. Drain the meat and reserve the marinade. Heat the dripping and fry the meat quickly on both sides. Remove from the pan and place in a 3-pint oblong 'Pyrex' casserole. Add the flour to the fat and cook slowly until lightly browned. Stir in the stock and marinade a little at a time and bring slowly to the boil, stirring constantly. Pour over the meat and cook at gas mark 2, 300°F (150°C) for $1\frac{1}{2}$ hours, then add the carrots and onions and cook for a further hour. To serve, adjust seasoning, arrange in the lid of the casserole dish and sprinkle with chopped parsley.

4 large herrings
salt and pepper
2½ oz (62 gm) butter
2 large Spanish onions, peeled
  and sliced

4 tomatoes, sliced
4 medium potatoes, peeled and
  thinly sliced
½ teaspoon (2.5 ml) dried chervil
¼ teaspoon (1.2 ml) fennel

Preheat oven to hot, gas mark 7, 425°F (220°C).

Remove herring heads with scissors and discard. Scrape each herring from tail to head with back of knife to remove scales. Slit fish along underside to tail and remove roe and blood vessel. Open each fish out and place cut side down on board. Press firmly along centre backbone to flatten fish. Turn over and remove backbone. Trim tails and fins with scissors, then rinse and pat dry on kitchen paper. Season with salt and pepper. Roll each herring up from tail to head. Grease a 2-pint round 'Pyrex' casserole with ½ oz (12 gm) butter. Put half the potatoes, half the onions and half the tomatoes into the casserole, and top with the remaining potatoes. Put the rolled herrings on top and cover with remaining tomatoes and onion. Season with salt and pepper, sprinkle with chervil and fennel and dot with remaining butter. Cover closely with lid and cook in centre of oven for 30–40 minutes. Remove cover and cook for a further 10 minutes, or until fish is cooked through and topping is browned.

# Pigeon casserole
## with redcurrants and sultanas

8 rashers lean bacon
1 oz (25 gm) fat for frying
1 large onion, chopped
$\frac{1}{2}$ pint (300 ml) stock
2 oz (50 gm) sultanas

4 oz (100 gm) redcurrants, fresh,
   tinned or frozen
salt and pepper
4 wood pigeons

Chop the bacon and fry in the hot fat, add the onion and cook until soft. Remove and drain and place in the bottom of a 3-pint oblong Opal 'Pyrex' casserole. Put the stock, sultanas, redcurrants and seasoning into the pan and bring to a fast boil. Place the pigeons in the casserole and pour the hot liquid over the top. Cook at gas mark 3, 325°F (170°C) for 3 hours.

# Mushroom and salmon casserole

4 salmon steaks
½ oz (12 gm) butter
salt and pepper
¼ pint (150 ml) white wine
water

1 teaspoon (5 ml) lemon juice
4 oz (100 gm) button mushrooms
4 slices of onion
1 teaspoon (5 ml) parsley,
  chopped

Place steaks in a 2½-pint oval 'Pyrex' casserole and dot butter over each steak. Season and grill until golden. Mix the wine with enough water to cover the steaks and heat gently in a saucepan. Add lemon juice and seasoning. Halve button mushrooms and place with onion rings in heaps on each steak. Cover steaks with liquid and place on the middle shelf of the oven at gas mark 4, 350°F (180°C) for 15–20 minutes. Sprinkle the top with parsley just before serving.

# Buttered grouse

1½ oz (37 gm) butter
2 slices bacon
1 tablespoon (15 ml) chopped onion

1 grouse
wineglass of red wine
1¼ fl oz (40 ml) brandy

Melt ½ oz (12 gm) of the butter and dice and fry the bacon. Put these together with onion into a 3-pint 'Pyrex' casserole. Brown the grouse in remaining butter and place in the casserole. Pour over the wine and brandy and cook at gas mark 4, 350°F (180°C) for 1 hour. Serve on a bed of fresh vegetables with creamed potatoes.

# Guinea fowl and celery casserole

2 guinea fowl
2 oz (50 gm) butter
4 heads of celery, trimmed and
   cleaned

$\frac{1}{4}$ pint (150 ml) white wine
$\frac{1}{4}$ pint (150 ml) stock
seasoning
$\frac{1}{4}$ pint (150 ml) single cream

Fry the guinea fowl all over in the hot butter. Remove from the pan and place in a 'Pyrex' chicken casserole. Split the celery in half lengthways and fry in the butter until golden then place in the casserole. Heat the wine, stock, seasoning and cream together, pour over the guinea fowl. Cover and cook at gas mark 3, 325°F (170°C) for 2 hours.

# Ginger gooseberry pie

12 oz (350 gm) shortcrust pastry
1 lb (450 gm) gooseberries
6 oz (150 gm) brown sugar

1 teaspoon (5 ml) ground ginger
beaten egg

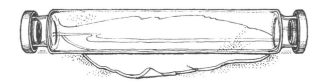

Roll out half the pastry and use it to line an 8½-in 'Pyrex' pie plate. Place the gooseberries, sugar and ginger in layers in the dish. Top with the remaining pastry, making a small hole in the top to allow the steam to escape. Decorate with shapes cut from pastry trimmings and glaze with beaten egg.

Bake at gas mark 5, 375°F (190°C) for 30 minutes.

1 oz (25 gm) caster sugar
½ pint (300 ml) milk
2 oz (50 gm) pudding rice

1 raspberry jelly
1 15 oz (450 gm) tin of raspberries

**Raspberry sauce**
4 oz (100 gm) raspberries,
   fresh or frozen

juice of 1 lemon
caster sugar

Place sugar, milk, and rice in a pan and bring to the boil. Simmer until rice is soft and the pudding becomes thicker. Leave to one side until cold. Make up the jelly to ½ pint (300 ml) with the juice from the raspberries and allow to cool. Combine with the cold rice pudding and leave to set. When almost set combine the drained raspberries and rice in a blender and pour into a 'Pyrex' jelly mould. Leave until firmly set. Unmould on to a flat plate and serve with raspberry sauce: beat the fresh or thawed frozen raspberries to a purée with the lemon and caster sugar to taste.

# Traditional Christmas pudding

*makes two 1 lb. ($\frac{1}{2}$-kilo) puddings*

4 oz (100 gm) self-rasing flour
$\frac{1}{2}$ level teaspoon (2.5 ml) mixed
  spice
4 oz (100 gm) suet
4 oz (100 gm) fresh white
  breadcrumbs
4 oz (100 gm) seedless raisins
4 oz (100 gm) sultanas
4 oz (100 gm) currants

2 oz (50 gm) mixed peel, chopped
2 oz (50 gm) soft brown sugar
4 oz (100 gm) black treacle
grated peel and juice of 1 orange
  and 1 lemon
2 small eggs, beaten
$\frac{1}{2}$ wineglass white rum
milk to mix if necessary
little icing sugar

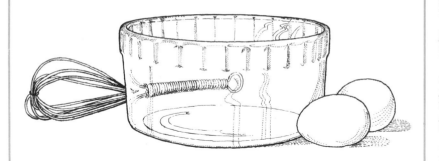

Sift flour and spice into bowl. Add suet, crumbs, dried fruit, peel and sugar. Mix thoroughly with treacle, grated peel and the juice of the orange and lemon, beaten eggs and rum. Stir in a little milk if mixture is very stiff and transfer to two well-greased 1-pint 'Pyrex' pudding basins. Cover securely with double thickness of greased greaseproof paper or aluminium foil and steam for 6 hours, topping up saucepan with extra boiling water as and when necessary. Leave until lukewarm, then turn out of basins. Wrap in clean foil when cold and store in a cool dry place until required. Before serving, transfer to greased basins, cover and steam for 2 hours. Dust lightly with icing sugar, and garnish with holly.